ACKNOWLEDGE[MENTS]

I would like to thank [...] inspiration.

Also my thanks go to [...] Walmsley and Jan Willia[ms ...] help and input.

My appreciation goes to Jared Jones who has captured the Duffy Divot image and bought the character to life.

Not least to the countless high handicap golfers, where I once belonged and to whom this book is dedicated. I hope it helps you to enjoy the wonderful game of golf.

Golf is a game in which you yell "Fore," score six and write down five.

CONTENTS

Introduction	4
Equipment	7
Course Management	13
Playing from the Rough	25
Par Three's	29
The Short Game	33
Putting	38
The Day Of Reckoning	49
Summary	51

Introduction

'If you drink don't drive. Don't even putt'... Dean Martin

At last a book full of great tips to help all you handicap golfers play better golf, without the need for extensive practice or major swing changes. In the following chapters I shall be suggesting tips and ideas to help you improve your golf.

I am not a golfing professional. I am no longer in the first flush of youth. I am overweight and cursed with persistent back pain, but I still play a mean game off eleven.

Before retiring I spent over forty years in show business as a comic and during that time I played hundreds of rounds of society golf, also numerous pro-ams, playing alongside club and touring professionals.

The last few years of my working life I was a golf club secretary, where I played the game with all types of players, consequently I have gleaned many tips and ideas and now as I have time to spare and as I'm becoming a bit of a fair-weather golfer I thought it might be an idea to pass on this knowledge in a light-hearted way, hence this book.

By the way I am not a teacher, if you wish to improve your golf swing and learn the mechanics of the game I recommend, you take lessons from a recognised PGA Teaching Professional.

Yes! We all want to hit the ball like Tiger Woods, Jack Nicklaus, Nick Faldo etc. but they are all gifted players, who have dedicated their lives to their sport, spending countless hours practising.

I have just read John Daly's autobiography [Golf - My Own Damn Way] and wild man or not, he still spent most of his childhood practising up to 8 hours a day, everyday.

To be a great player you have to be gifted with perfect timing, this is something that cannot be taught, you either have it or you don't.

90% of all golfers don't have the time or the inclination to practice, 50% or more only play about once a month and maybe not at all during the winter months.

But all the instruction books or videos state the only way to improve your game is to practice. I agree, if you want to become a low handicap player, but the guy who only plays once a month, just wants to shave a few shots off his game (so he can win the money for a change).

So what's so different about this book from the countless others out there in the market place relating to golf I hear you say?

My intention is not to write an instruction book per se; although there will be a few swing suggestions, it's more a collection of tips and thoughts to help the higher handicap player achieve better scores without the need to practice.

I was once a high handicap player (a complete and utter Duffy Divot) until I opened my eyes and began to use the tips and thoughts contained in this book.

When I put these collected tips and thoughts into practice I was no longer a Duffy Divot and my eyes were opened to a wide range of possibilities.

Everyone replaces their divot after a perfect approach shot.

Wife says to her husband. "If I died would you remarry?"

Husband answers. "Maybe"

Wife; "Would you marry another lady golfer?"

Husband; "Maybe"

Wife; "But you wouldn't let her use my clubs, would you?"

Husband; "No Dear! She's left handed."

Equipment

"The most exquisitely satisfying act in the world of golf is that of throwing a club..." Henry Longhurst

Let us face facts, you can't buy a golf game no matter how much you spend, but you can improve what game you have with the right equipment.

Many high handicap golfers (Duffy Divots) by not fully understanding the nuances of golf are hindering their game by playing with the wrong clubs. Often they have bought their clubs second-hand, or borrowed an old set from a friend.

They spend time boasting about what a good deal they struck; not knowing that the clubs they have may be totally unsuitable for their particular requirements.

For example: they never thought to check the tension of the shaft. For high handicap players it should be at the least regular, for the older player and the very high handicapper, extra flex would be advisable, stiff shafts are only for very low handicap players.

Although the book is specifically aimed at the higher handicap player, these tips can be of help to any golfer regardless of their standard. I have seen numerous Duffy Divots, they have a complete mish-mash of clubs, all different makes, some steel shafts, some graphite, a complex mix of stiff and regular shafts and they wonder why they can't hit the ball with any consistency.

When you read this it sounds so obvious, but there are hundreds and thousands of golfers out there; you probably know one that has a bag full of allsorts, let's hope it's not you.

If this is you then now is the time for change. Golf is a hard enough game without the added problem of playing with the wrong equipment.

Another way to help your game is to make sure your grips are not worn or shiny. When you consider the grip is the only part of the club that attaches to your body via your hands you would think it advisable to have the best adhesion you can; you wouldn't drive your car on completely bald tyres would you, do you get my drift?

It also amazes me how many Duffy Divots I see who never clean their clubs after a shot, they pick the club out of the bag covered in mud, weeds and who knows what else and wonder why they can't hit a good shot, it beggars belief!

Tip number one: Check the tension on the shafts of your clubs. In a perfect world you need a matching set of regular tension graphite shafts. I suggest graphite because they are more forgiving and give a bit more whip at the bottom of the swing, if you prefer steel okay, but get the right tension.

There are many golf outlets these days that sell clubs at very reasonable prices, with expert assistants to help you. For only a few pounds more have the "loft & lie" of the clubs adjusted to your swing.

Over the top you say, but it depends on how much you want to improve. I had the loft & lie adjusted on my clubs a couple of years ago and it made an immediate improvement to my ball striking. I wish I had done it sooner. As I say, they can often do it while you wait and it's not expensive.

The simple way to check if you need to have your clubs adjusted is to take your normal stance with an iron and see if the toe of the club or the heel is off the ground. The club should lie flat from the toe to the heel, if not you need to have the adjustment.

This may also be achieved by changing your hand position on the club grip (either moving hands up or down the grip), to ensure that the club is flat from toe to heel, experiment for yourself.

Tip number two: There are countless drivers and 3 woods in the market place from over £500 to £20. My advice is buy what you can afford, the £500 club should stay on the rack for Duffy Divot, a very low handicapper might get a further 10 yards with those wonder clubs but for Duffy Divot it would be a complete waste of money.

At the other end of the spectrum, don't go for the very cheap clubs, they do not work and don't last very long, and I speak from experience.

As I say, pay what you can afford. The best method is to make a visit to one of the golf outlets, make sure that it has a driving range and try before you buy.

Search out woods that are last year's model. With regards to the driver you need a loft of no less than 10.5, the more loft the better and also get the largest head you can, they not only give you a larger sweet spot hitting area, they look good behind the ball which gives you more confidence, so that's ideal for our Duffy Divot.

If you have a limited budget, plump for a good 3 wood, the difference in yardage is minimal and they are easier to hit.

Remember whenever possible always try out the clubs before you buy them.

Tip number three: Always take the club you are replacing with you to the testing area, because most range balls are of a poorer quality, so you do not get the same distance, so if you compare the new with the old club you will know if it is any better.

Tip number four: Hybrid clubs are a modern innovation with which I heartily concur. Hybrid clubs are much easier to hit out of the rough as well as the fairway, they get the ball up high and seem to go further than the equivalent iron.

They are the ideal club for Duffy Divot, they replace the 3 and 4 irons, which most Duffy Divots find hard to hit, and if you like them you can go down further (if they went down as far as a 9 iron equivalent I would have that as well).

Remember anything that helps is okay, as long as you have no more than 14 clubs in your bag.

Tip number five: Buy the most appropriate balls; don't buy the most expensive but not the cheapest. Buy lake balls or refurbished balls, they are perfectly adequate for Duffy

Divot (however we all discover our own personal favourites over time).

Remember pay only what you can afford to lose.

So far you might think it is all outlay and as I stated earlier, you can't buy a decent golf game. But by the same token, you can't play a decent game without the right equipment, so it's a compromise; buy what you think you can afford and that will give you at least a fair chance to improve.

One birdie is a hot streak

My game is so bad at the moment, I had to have my ball retriever re-gripped.

Course Management

"Give me golf clubs, fresh air and a beautiful partner, and you can keep the clubs and fresh air..." Jack Benny

As I stated in the introduction, I have played hundreds of society golf rounds with complete hackers to accomplished players. The first thing you notice with the Duffy Divots of this world is their complete lack of golf course management. Often arriving on the first tee completely unprepared to play…

They stand on the tee and hit at the ball as hard as they can, usually with the wrong club, often with no game plan and no idea of where they are going.

Swing deficiencies will mean that Duffy Divots either slice or hook the ball (with no particular consistency) and then wonder why they cannot hit the fairway.

I'll take the time to remind you that you really should see a PGA Teaching Professional; many will do a free assessment of your swing and leave you with a few thoughts. I can heartily recommend this approach, I had my swing assessed and within 10 minutes I was given some invaluable guidance and the next time on the golf course I kept in it the short grass and used the same ball for the whole round.

Find a Duffy Divot Accredited PGA Professional at www.duffydivot.com

The quickest way to get your handicap down and lose shots on every round is to improve your "**Course Management**".

Whenever you play a new course (and even your home track) be aware and look, whenever possible, at other holes and greens as you pass them by. Take in as much information as possible, where bunkers are situated, flag positions, slope on greens. On many courses the fairways run parallel, try to observe par threes especially, because if the flag is at the front or back this can be a difference of two clubs.

OK now let's play an imaginary hole together. This is a par four straight, 410 yards long (from the yellow tee) with trouble on the right, bunkers on the left at 250 yards and one across the fairway 30 yards from the front of the green, bunkers left and right beside the green, Stroke index 6.

Let's imagine Duffy Divot hits all his shots with a slice, if you hook the ball or you're left handed just reverse this advice.

The number one rule in the art of course management is, if you have shots use them sensibly. Before starting each round set yourself a goal of trying to score 2 Stableford points on each hole. If you do not understand the Stableford points system, it means with the aid of our handicap we are trying to get a net par on each hole, it will not be easy but it

Stableford Scoring System – Duffy Divot's Guide, at www.duffydivot.com

is attainable, if you go about it in the right way.

If you really want to get your handicap down you have to be very honest with yourself. Most Duffy Divots think they hit the ball further than they actually do; I would say most Duffy Divots hit their drives no more than 200 yards maximum, in some cases less than that.

Next time you play, pace out three or four of your drives to get an average, you will probably be surprised how short they are.

It really helps your course management when you know how far you really do hit it, by the same token if you are a long hitter, fine, but know your distances. Why is it so important I hear you ask, read on, all will be made clear. Now you know the average distance of your drive you can set about making your 2 points.

First take a look at the layout of the hole, we have trouble down the right and bunkers at 250 yards on the left, and we hit the ball with a slice, (a slice is when the ball moves in the air from left to right as it loses its momentum, a hook goes the other way).

I could get all technical here about how to cure a slice. A slice is caused because the clubface is cutting across the ball from out to in or right to left at impact, thereby imparting left to right spin on the ball which makes it go to the right. You can play with a slice and still make a good score as long as you remember to play with the slice or hook in mind.

Now here's where we change your mind set. Most Duffy Divots just walk up to the tee, pick out the driver, tee it up in the middle of the tee area, blast away as hard as they can and then watch it sail into the trees on the right and wonder why it always happens to them.

The first thing to remember is to play with your brain and not your brawn. We have established you hit your drives around the 200 yards mark and they go left to right. So we tee the ball up as far right of the teeing ground as possible, we stand behind the ball and look down the left hand side of the fairway beyond the 200 yards, as I said previously there are bunkers at 250 yards.

Take a mental picture on the line of the left hand side of these bunkers and follow it back to your ball, now find a mark about two feet to a yard in front of your ball on the line to the edge of the bunkers.

We now address the ball, lining up your club head on that mark you have in your peripheral vision. The aim of the exercise is to start your ball over that mark towards the bunkers on the left hand side of the fairway with the flight of the ball going away from all the trouble down the right, also you now have the complete width of the fairway to land in and not 50% when you aim down the middle.

You are not going to land in the bunkers, they are too far. When your slice starts to take over in the flight of your ball it will land in the fairway and if you hit that shot in a hundred where it goes dead straight it will still be in the fairway. All professional players hit their shots with a fade or draw so they have the entire fairway to play with.

Tip number six: The finding of a mark two feet in front of your ball is a useful aid. I read this in a Jack Nicholas book and if it's good enough for him it should certainly help a Duffy Divot. I recommend you carry out this drill on every single shot you take (the mark you select can be anything visible).

It helps with your alignment but more importantly it can improve your swing. When striking the ball try and aim the club head over the spot you have chosen, this will not only send the ball in the right direction but will also straighten out your swing plane, which in turn will cut down on the slice or hook you have, because the club is going down the line of the ball flight and not across it.

Tip number seven: When you play your shot and this is the most important tip I will give in this entire book, only hit the ball with no more than 85% of your full power.

Ernie Els has a perfect swing and he says he never hits the ball flat out, the reason being that when you try to hit flat out you over swing and lose your timing.

I'm sure at some time during your golfing career you have had the situation where you are laying up in front of a pond or lake, so you hit the ball with a nice smooth swing and the ball flies away much further than normal straight into the water.

It's not rocket science is it!

Tip number eight: There are only two occasions when you can handle the ball prior to making a shot (except of course for winter rules); they are when you tee off and when putting, which I shall come to later.

So let's once again take full advantage of the situation and use our brains. When teeing off, place the ball on the tee with the manufacturer's logo at the back of the ball, so when you focus on the ball to make your shot you look at the logo on the back of the ball.

Remember to look only at the back of the ball, not the complete ball, because after all is said and done, that's the part of the ball you connect with. (You know it makes sense).

Just as a point of etiquette, you should always, even in a friendly round, tell your playing partners the make and number ball you are playing, simply because it can save any embarrassment later if you have two or more playing with the same make and number ball (if you have to use another ball because one has been lost you should also inform your playing partners).

Tip number nine: On the subject of balls, if you are playing on a cold day, keep a ball of the same make and number in you trouser pocket, and exchange it every alternative hole, a warmer ball travels further than a cold one. This tip was acquired on a Scottish golfing holiday a while ago.

Tip number ten: To help you play better and improve your round, ask your playing partners in a polite and pleasant manner if they would mind watching out for your ball.

Golf being a game played by gentlemen, they will always agree as this eliminates the lifting of your head to follow the ball and also speeds up your round because you (and they) are not searching in vain miles from where it has landed.

So we have played our tee shot, I am leaving it to you as to which club you play as long as you realise that the driver is the hardest club to hit within your bag.

If you watch professional golf on television as I do, you will know that the statistic for overall driving accuracy is only 60%, so if the professionals miss fairways 40% of the time with their driver, what chance has a Duffy Divot! I would always suggest the 3 wood for a Duffy Divot, as I said earlier, easier to hit and the difference in distance is minimal.

Let us move on: we have played our tee shot and if everything has gone to plan we should be on the fairway, approximately 200 yards from the tee which means we are 210 yards from the centre of the green.

The biggest temptation for a Duffy Divot is to try and emulate his playing partners. Big mistake!

So okay they have knocked their ball 40 yards past you and will be able to go for the green with their next shot, but you have the advantage, you have two shots in hand, you have reached less than halfway with your drive, so what makes you think you can make the green with a lesser club than your tee shot, use your brain not your brawn, play with your handicap in mind.

As I said, there is a fairway cross bunker 30 yards from the front of the green, that means we have 170 yards to the bunker. Everyone has a rough idea how far they hit each club, another amazing statistic is that professionals admit that even when they have played a below par round, ***they only hit eight to ten perfect shots in any given round.***

So what chance has a Duffy Divot hitting a perfect shot? You have to play the percentages. Go up one more club than you think you need. Next we repeat the routine we did on the tee. Stand behind the ball and pick a spot in the distance beyond the 160 yards on the left side of the fairway, find the spot in front of your ball. As before hit the ball with the club head going over the spot we have chosen at no more than 85% of your full power.

All things being equal we should now be in the middle of the fairway short of the cross bunker. The next step is to get on to the green as close to the flag as possible. I know this sounds pretty obvious but it's amazing how many Duffy Divots do not achieve this task.

After we have worked out the distance, like before, choose one club up.

Tip number eleven: Do not, I repeat do not, aim at the flag, you pick a spot over or at the back of the green 10 feet to the left of the flag. Why? I hear you say!

Because like before, we are using our brains. You hit the ball with a slice so by all accounts it's going to go right, so over the 70/80 yards we have to the pin it should go no further than 10 feet right, of course the further away from the hole we are, the more we aim to the left of the flag. But for now 10 feet left is enough, now if your ball goes badly right you will still only be 10 feet right of the flag. If it goes straight you will only be 10 feet left of the flag. Also by taking one club more, you are sure to be up to the flag, you rarely see a Duffy Divot pass the flag.

If you have followed my advice, you should now be on the green for three shot close to the flag and you are now putting for a gross par, or a net eagle. Even if you three putt, (I will come to putting tips later on in the book), you will have achieved your aim by scoring 2 points, you have taken 6 shots you receive 2 shots which means a net par 4 = 2 points. Obviously if you can take fewer than three putts your score will improve accordingly.

Tip number twelve: Try and repeat your practice swing when you are hitting the ball for real. When you take a practice swing you don't actually hit at the ball because there is no ball there to hit, but when it comes to playing your shot for real, most players have a tendency to strike at the ball. **<u>WRONG.</u>**

This causes all sorts of faults, just try and swing the club in one nice smooth arc where the ball gets in the way, rather than hitting at it. You will find you make a much better contact and the ball will fly further and straighter.

There's an old saying in golf ***"Keep your head down"***. I'm sure you have heard it many times; in fact you have probably said it yourself after a particularly bad shot. Surprisingly this is not as common a fault as people think. They use this as an excuse but it is more likely that they did something else wrong.

If you have asked, as I suggested earlier, your playing partners to watch out for your ball you have no need to raise your head prior to contact.

Trying consciously to keep one's head down leads to tension and tension is a big ***NO NO*** in golf.

Almost all Duffy Divots and many other golfers play with too much tension in their game. You watch them grip the club and you can see the veins sticking out on the backs of their hands and up their arms.

They are frightened to hold the club lightly because they think it is going to fly out of their grip if they don't. Trust me, it will not, the human body is an amazing machine, if you hold the club lightly with no tension in your hands and arms, when you swing to the top of your backswing and down again, the brain tells the muscles to tighten just sufficiently for the club not to fly off in all directions.

When I first left school I had an apprenticeship working in an engineering factor, One of the jobs I did was working with the Blacksmith, he taught me how to use a hammer and like all beginners, I held it far to tightly. He told me to hold the hammer like you would a baby bird in your hand, I followed his advice and at no time did I lose grip of the hammer, I also did not go home each night with an aching arm.

So try and hold the club lightly, if you are not sure just try a few practice swings, you might surprise yourself.

The Glory Shot

What is the glory shot I hear you ask? This is a shot that is beyond your ability and which you should not try, such as playing over a lake which is at the very upper limit of your range, over bunkers, out of trees etc.

There is an imp on your shoulder who's saying "Go on go for it, are you a man or a mouse"? You know you shouldn't listen to him but you do and once in a hundred tries it comes off. Now you are hooked and every time you get yourself in a similar position, you go for the glory shot, because all you can remember is the one time you pulled it off and not the 99% of times when you didn't.

Reading this you know the sensible thing to do is play the percentage shot and not the stupid shot.

I have a friend who is still a true Duffy Divot and when we have this conversation regarding glory shots he says, "It's more fun going for the impossible".

Now I think it's more fun to win and pick up the money, but I'm a winner and not a loser. I want the other players to have to play better than me and not me give-away shots because of my stupidity.

You can hit a 2-acre fairway 10% of the time, and a 2-inch branch 90% of the time.

 Two long time golfers were standing over looking a river. One golfer looked at the other and said. "Look at those idiots fishing in the rain

Playing from the Rough

"Most people swing as if they are digging for worms..."
David Leadbetter

Although this book is aimed at helping you round in a lower score without the need to practice, there is a time when everyone lands in the rough.

This is another area where by using commonsense and not the gung-ho attitude of Duffy Divot we can shave shots off your score.

Lesson number one, get the ball back in play on the short grass by the quickest and shortest route possible. If you are deep in the trees don't aim at a gap twenty five yards in front of you which is only two feet wide. Don't listen to the imp on your shoulder, play the sensible shot. These rescue shots are easy to play if you approach them in the right way.

Tip number thirteen: I use this all the time with these types of shots; the advice is to take an eight iron and play the ball off your back foot. At the address, have your hands slightly ahead of the ball then when you take your shot look at the front of the ball and not the back of it.

This encourages you to hit the ball first and not stub the ground behind the ball, also this is one occasion where it is vital that you keep your head down whilst watching the front of the ball, until after the shot has been played.

Tip number fourteen: If you are deep in the trees and there is no short way out and your only choice is the two foot gap twenty five yards away, my advice is to aim at the left tree (if you tend to slice) or the right tree (if you tend to hook).

It takes a bit of nerve to do this, but come on be honest with yourself, whenever you are presented with this problem you aim at the gap and always hit the tree.

So it makes sense that by aiming at the trees you may just go through the gap, go on try it.

Semi-Rough

When playing out of the rough you should let your common sense dictate and not your ego.

If you have bought the hybrid clubs as I suggested, they are perfect for light semi-rough. If it is deeper then play the right club to get you back on the fairway, forget distance think fairway.

Address the ball once again off the back foot. Grip two inches down the shaft of the club, cock the wrist earlier in the back swing and hit the ball with a descending blow, try if you can to strike the ball first and not the grass, it will come out as sweet as a nut.

The number one priority when playing from the rough is to get the ball back in play in as few strokes as possible, I repeatedly see Duffy Divots trying to hit long irons or wood shots out of the rough, all that happens is they hit the ball a few yards, have a good swear then repeat the same scenario again and again...

Once again I remind you, take advantage of the shots you have and use them wisely and don't throw them away by attempting the impossible. Take a lofted club and get the ball back on the fairway by the quickest and shortest route possible.

Yes I agree! Tiger can hit a six iron from 190 yards out of deep rough over trees, across a lake and onto the green five feet from the stick, but look in the mirror Duffy Divot "You ain't no Tiger". Face facts and get the ball back into play.

Fairway Bunkers

Once again these are usually a problem for a Duffy Divot, because at the risk of repeating myself, they try to play too ambitiously and not within their capabilities.

Your number one priority is to get the ball out, forget distance, think fairway. The height of the bunker shoulder is one factor that dictates which club you play.

The higher the shoulder the higher the club number. Another factor is the proximity of your ball to the front or back of the bunker, don't go for distance you'll duff it by hitting the sand because you swing too hard at the ball, or hit the bunker shoulder in front of you because you did not have enough loft.

Play the shot once again off your back foot. Shuffle your feet into the sand to get a solid base, this is another time when looking at the front of the ball helps to get a good clean strike by hitting the ball first and not the sand, unlike greenside bunkers where you hit the sand first, I'll go into this shot later in greater detail in the short game chapter.

Confidence evaporates in the presence of water.

A guy is at the driving range having a heck of a day.

Everything thing he tries to hit he tops, balls only going about 20' and burning worms the whole way. Finally disgusted, he turns to the pro on the range and mutters," If I don't connect with this one, I'm gonna jump in that lake and drown myself!"

Pro looks at him and says " I don't think you can do it."

"Why not?" He asks.

Pro says "I don't think you can keep your head down that long!"

Par Three's

"I'm hitting the woods just great, but I'm having terrible time getting out of them..." Harry Tofcano

Par Three holes are very good holes for the high handicapper; these are Duffy Divot scoring holes.

No matter what your handicap is, if you can play the par three holes well you usually end up with a good Stableford score for your round.

Most courses include at least three par threes. The reason they are scoring holes is because even with a bad tee shot you should be on the green for two.

Try and take no more that two putts, then you will have achieved your goal of a net par (or two Stableford points). Mostly you will be receiving a handicap point on these holes and in some cases maybe two. That's the time take to full advantage. There's nothing more demoralising for your better handicap players partners! as when you walk off a green and tell them to mark your score down, four for three points, or three for four, or even a three for five.

Their comments can be really quite therapeutic to hear.

But we have to score those points first, so how do we go about it? As I have already said on more than one occasion, we use our little grey cells. Fault number one with all Duffy Divots, they under-club on all par threes.

Be honest with yourself, when was the last time you went over the back of the green on a par three with your tee shot?

That alone should tell you something.

Secondly when did you last stand on the tee and really study the hole? I mean take it all in and not just a general look. Did you for example notice where all the bunkers were? If they were on both sides and at the front, was there a side with no bunkers, were there bunkers at the back?

The reason you should take all this information on board is that it determines the type of shot you are going to attempt. You will find that the majority of par threes are designed with all the bunkers at the front and either side, very rarely at the back.

So if there are no bunkers at the back this is the safest part of the green to aim for.

As I said earlier, most Duffy Divots under-club on par three holes. So firstly, after you have determined the yardage and you have a club in mind that you feel will get you there, add one to that straight away, why I hear you say?

Your club yardage determination is a result of flight and run on the ball. When hitting into a par three green over bunkers we need more flight which means more club. Also another fact to compute is that when you hit a ball off a tee peg it is a recognized fact that all golfers lose one club length distance (i.e. approximately 10 yards), and if you hit the ball with only 85% of your power the correct club is two more than you originally thought you needed, (even before taking into account if there's no wind or elevation to consider).

So let's play the hole. Duffy Divot take your time never rush at golf it's not a race, as the famous American golfer Ben Hogan said 'smell the flowers'.

Study the hole, look where all the trouble is, if there are bunkers at the front or right then play away from them. It's the same with water, deep rough and trees, try and take them out of the equation. Tee up depending on your type of shot (Slice or Hook) on the side of the tee as before so the ball is always heading away from the trouble.

Tee the ball a good inch to two inches off the ground with the logo at the back of the ball. Don't I repeat don't, do as the professionals do, tee it just off the ground, because this only encourages you to hit it fat (when you hit the ground behind the ball first).

This encourages you to make a nice sweeping motion with a long follow through down the line of the mark about two or three feet in front of the ball (as suggested earlier). The point of aim is determined by where the flag and trouble are. As previously mentioned when playing a wedge shot into the par four hole, it's best to rarely aim straight at the flag (especially if you have a slice or a hook).

We are not going to get into taking contours of the green into consideration this is just too complicated, I know the professionals do, so they are below the flag as they say, but it is cutting down your limitations to, in some cases, a ten foot margin, (hello)! We just want get onto the green by avoiding all the trouble. Take the ten foot method again depending where the flag is, if it's close to a bunker aim a little further away, it's much easier putting than playing out of bunkers.

Tip number fifteen: On long par three holes swallow your pride and do not try and fly one all the way. Take an iron and play short, then on the green for two, most long par three holes have a low stroke index, so you will be receiving two shots, ***DUFFY DIVOT - USE THEM.***

Notice in men's changing room of a famous Jewish London Golf Club. 'Would Members refrain from picking up lost balls until they have stopped rolling'.

What are the four worst words you could hear during a game of golf? 'It's still your turn'.

The Short Game

"Golf is deceptively simple yet endlessly complicated..."
Arnold Palmer

This department of the game is where all Duffy Divots can gain a lot of shots back by using commonsense and by playing the right shot at the right time, plus at the risk of repetition, playing within Duffy Divot's limitations. The objective is to try and turn three shots into two.

Approach Shots

We will start with the short approach shots onto the green. To make sure not to leave the ball short, aim at the top of the flag; this will give you the required distance.

If you have to go over a bunker onto the green and the flag is your side leaving you little room to land the ball, the shot is the ***'Flop Shot'***. This is a shot where the ball goes high almost straight up and lands like a butterfly with sore feet.

It needs to be played with confidence. It's better played out of low rough (on tight cut grass or off a fairway; it's a much more difficult shot).

If you have any doubts then play the standard pitch shot, even if it means playing away from the flag, as I keep saying, play with your shots in mind and avoid bunkers etc.

The flop shot is played as follows; firstly there are specialist clubs for this shot, wedges with a 60 and more degree of loft, but it can easily be played with your sand wedge.

Address the ball with a slightly open stance, line the ball off the inside of your front foot, place the club on the ground behind the ball with the back of the club flat on the ground, the face of the club pointing at the sky and slightly open. Now grip the club as it lies, take a full backswing and attempt to hit the ground about an inch behind the ball and sweep the bottom hand through and under the ball with a full follow-through. Keep your shoulders, hips and knees pointing slightly left of the target, try not to lift your body up during the stroke.

The speed of the hit is about one and half times faster than you think it will be. After a few attempts you will soon get the hang of it, it's a great shot to have in the bag.

Chipping

A lot of players no matter what their standard seem to have problems with chipping.

Tip number sixteen: For this precise shot; always choose a club that will get the ball running across the green as quickly as possible, don't play with a wedge for every shot. To stop the chunk shot where you hit the ground behind the ball, firstly make sure you do not lift your head looking to see if you have played the right shot, this makes you shoulders drop hence chunk behind the ball.

Try standing closer to the ball, lifting the heel of the club whilst hitting the ball more with the toe of the club to deliver a controllable chip shot.

Tip number seventeen: This is the best tip in the world which I have mentioned before, but you must do this especially on this particular shot. Look at the front of the ball, this ensures a good clean strike on the back of the ball, I can't emphasise this enough. A good chip can turn three shots into two every time.

There are specialist clubs on the market called 'Chippers', they have about the same loft as a seven iron, and you are supposed to play them like a putter. I feel they are a great club when you get used to them, but they take a bit of getting used to because you need to move your hands to increase and decrease the loft of the club as required.

If you feel you can't come to terms using your irons with this shot, it might be an idea to invest in a 'Chipper'.

Tip number eighteen: If you are only just off the green, use a 5 wood or one of your equivalent hybrid clubs. Hold the club well down the shaft and play the shot as you would if playing with your putter; this gets the ball airborne just enough to let you land it on the green and let it run out to the flag.

Texas Wedge

If you don't know what a Texas Wedge is, it's your putter. If the grass is not too long and you are no more than say ten yards off the green, there's nothing wrong in taking your putter, obviously you have to hit a little harder than when on the green. To help with this stroke move your hands a little ahead of the ball, this encourages you to hit the ball with top spin so that it runs over the top of the grass (and doesn't dig in losing you momentum).

You will find an average putt is generally always better than a poor chip.

You need to appreciate the extra energy provided when using this club for chip shots.

Bunker Shot

Another big fear for Duffy Divot is the green-side bunker. Although the teaching and professional world state that this is a simple shot, I don't agree and like most people, have had my troubles with this shot. You have to play this shot with confidence and that's the key to this shot, confidence.

Again we can cheat on this shot sometimes; the main aim is to get the ball out. Unlike the professionals we are not going to be able to leave it stone dead. ***Oh how we wish!***

Let's just get it on the green and use our shots sensibly. If the bunker wall is not steep but quite flat there is no reason why we can't putt the ball out, it's not against the rules, but like the wedge you must not touch the sand with your club behind the ball. If the bunker has only a small lip you can play a chip shot off your back foot, so you hit the ball first and not the sand'.

If the only shot out is a proper bunker shot, shuffle your feet in an open position into the sand so that you get a solid base, bend your knees and remember to stay down, don't be tempted to lift your head to see if you have got it out because if you do you won't.

This shot is played exactly like the flop shot, the only difference is that you enter the sand a little further back about four inches.

Long Bunker Shots
This shot presents problems for golfers of all abilities; even the professionals say it's the hardest shot in golf.

Tip number nineteen: Just because you are in a bunker you do not have to play a sand iron, you can use a nine or even an eight, depending the distance required. This of course is dependent where the ball lies in the bunker and the height of the bunker lip in front of you.

I missed a hole in one yesterday by six shots.

If you have difficulty meeting new people, try picking up someone else's ball.

Putting

"Golf balls are attracted to water as unerringly as the eye of a middle-age man to a female bosom..." Michael Green

All champion players are good putters; they all hit the ball about the same tee to green, so it's the player who makes the fewest putts over the week who usually wins the tournament.

So I cannot emphasise the importance of putting. If you can eliminate those three putts at most holes you will save yourself a whole stack of shots.

There have been many pundits in the past that have said 'Putting is a game within a game', basically they are right, more shots are lost and gained on the greens than any other part of the course. You have only to listen to the chatter from fellow golfers in the clubhouse bemoaning how many three putts they had, rather than saying how many times it took them to play three shots or more to the par four holes. They know that's where they lost shots to their playing companions.

So when walking onto a putting green try and get a general feel for the lie of the land. Sometimes the surrounding ground can give you a misleading view of the slopes of the green, where the surrounding area slopes one way, but the actual green goes in another direction.

So when you walk up to your ball, if it's at the back of the green or to one side, approach the ball from the opposite side of the flag to your ball.

To get a feel of the slope if any, walk from the flag to your ball; this gives you a sense of the distance through your feet.

This may sound stupid, but don't knock it until you try it. This will only take you a few seconds. Don't act like the professionals where they wait until it's their turn then circumnavigate their putts, consult with their caddies; no wonder it takes them over five hours to play as a two ball *(Ridiculous)*.

The best way to approach the putting is to break it down into the three putts you are going to face, the long putt, the mid-range putt and the short putt.

The Long Putt
Try and give yourself only one thought on each putt. The two main items of the equation are speed and line, but most times you spend so much time studying the line you get the speed wrong, or visa versa.

Most greens in the United Kingdom are relatively flat so they do not have 'massive borrows' on them. Also the grass used is less grainy when compared to more exotic types found in the United States of America, South Africa et al.

So my advice on long putts is to think speed rather than direction. Most books recommend you to visualise a 1 metre circle around the hole and try to get inside that, it's good advice. This is of course where you do not have a massive borrow on the green. If you do, look at the next paragraph and it will help you. If you can get it close it's taking the pressure off the next putt so you will start two putting.

The Mid-Range Putt

I call these the *"Money Making Putts"*. If you are able to sink four or five of these types of putts during a round you will be in the money. I'm referring to those six to ten footers.

Tip number twenty: to help you make these money putts. ***(The Plumbob Method).*** Stand about ten feet behind your ball, take your putter and hold it by the top of its grip in one hand, and let it hang down vertically. Line the putter shaft on your ball through to the hole, close one eye and look through your dominant eye.

Hand dominance does not always correlate with eye dominance. Most people automatically use their dominant eye when looking through a camera lens or a telescope.

If there is a contour on the green, the shaft of the club will now be left or right of the hole.

Find a spot in front of you within your peripheral vision to aim the ball over relative to the distance your putter shaft is indicating that it is 'outside the hole' and play down that line.

This once again stops the dual-thinking scenario; we have our line so now all we need to think about is speed. If we can get the speed right we have a more than average chance that

---

Commit to your line - Duffy Divot's Practical line on successful putting, at www.duffydivot.com

we are going to make the putt. If we miss we are still close enough to make the next putt. My theory is that speed is more important than borrow.

On these putts think of six to ten inches for the ball to finish behind the hole. There is nothing worse than leaving a birdie putt or any putt inches in front of the hole, I will always remember once playing in Scotland many years ago, (back in the days when you had to play with a Caddy.

This weather-beaten old-boy said to me when I left a putt short 'Laddie yon hole will ne'er come to yee' and I thought how true in many situations.

I have just been watching 'The Accenture Match Play Championship 2008', which surprise, surprise, Tiger Woods won.

During the telecast Butch Harmon, Tiger's ex. coach said "One of the reasons Tiger is such a great champion is because he putts so well, the speed of his putts are so good, each putt looks whether he misses or not as if it's going in the hole."

I have been watching golf since it has been shown on television and I can honestly say I have never seen anybody sink as many mid-range putts as Tiger Woods and it's all down to speed. So try the *(The Plumbob Method)* I'm sure it will help you.

While we are talking about putting and with reference to Duffy Divot (usually a casual golfer who is not a golf club member but one who plays at a different course each time) do take time to gauge the speed of greens and make time to warm up on the practice greens before your round.

If you are a club member and play the same course all the time you become accustomed and aware of your home greens. However they can vary depending where the green keeper decides to place the holes on that particular day.

The Short Putts

On short putts and I mean three foot and under this, the best way of getting the ball into the hole.

Tip number twenty one: Try whenever possible to take any break out of the putt, this means don't give the hole away. Aim inside the cup and hit the ball firmly enough so that it keeps a straight line and which is not deviated by the slope on the green.

The best way is to pick a spot on the back of the cup and aim your ball at that spot. Also, all makes of balls have the maker's name printed on them.

To help alignment and encourage a smooth stroke, place your ball with the maker's name aiming at the spot you have chosen.

Most modern putters have alignment lines on the back of the putter, so you line up the putter's lines with the line on the ball on the spot at the back of the hole. A nice firm stroke and bingo, ball holed!

You can purchase a device that helps you place a line on the ball's equator which makes lining up putts even easier. If you watch golf on television you will see that most of the pros are using a suitably marked ball.

Tip number twenty two taken from the professional players, is to try and visualise the ball going into the hole, it does work.

Do try this method especially when short putting.

Either the maker's name or draw your own line (it's allowed in the rules)

Duffy Divot's Ball Marking Guide, at www.duffydivot.com

Putters

Most Duffy Divots have been playing with the same putter since they first started. If it works for you and I mean really works then you are indeed blessed, but I will guarantee the majority are playing with the wrong type of putter for their size, style or course.

As you are aware, there are hundreds of different types of putters now available ranging from ten pounds to hundreds of pounds.

Which is the right one for you? That's like asking which horse is going win the Derby. So what's the answer? we all know the answer, try different ones out, but as I said in the introduction, this book is aimed at the chap who does not have the time to practice and spend countless hours on the practice green trying out different putters.

The shame is, putting is half the game and you only use one club to play it with, so it would make sense that you have the right one. I know guys that have spent hundreds of pounds on different drivers but still have a two-bob putter that they bought from a boot sale.

Then on the reverse side, there are guys who have bought these new two-ball putters for well over a hundred pounds and they are completely the wrong type for their style of putting.

The basic rule is find one that feels comfortable in your hands. It's strange but you can spend just a few minutes in a golf shop picking up putters and even without a ball, some putters feel better in our hands than others. In a perfect world it's better to try out your putter before purchase. The trouble is that there are so many different styles and lengths on the market.

Once upon a time you only had the normal length putter. Length is very important, most poor putters play with a putter that is too long for them; it prevents them from letting their arms hang down in a natural way to form a triangle with their shoulders.

There are now various shape and sizes on the market, you have the belly, the broom handle, grips where you place your hands side by side as against one above the other.

It's very rare you see society type golfers using the belly or broom handle style putters and yet you watch the professionals and they are changing putters virtually on a daily basis, Monty, Darren Clark and Sergio Garcia, just to name a few seem to play each round with a different putter. The reason of course is because they know if they don't make the money putts they will not be playing at the weekend.

In many cases *'The Yips'* that's what it's called, has been the finish of their careers for some fine golfers. One of the higher profile sufferers was commentator Peter Allis, in fact it got so bad he had the number plate on his car changed to PUTT 3.

Bernard Langer experienced them three times, until his career was rescued by the broom handled putter popularised by Sam Torrance and Bruce Lietzhe.

As some players get older they develop the putting shakes. A large number of senior players on the Champions Tour now use the broom handled putter. So golfers of all standards are continually searching for that magic tool. As I said earlier, Tiger is the best money putter of all time, but it will be interesting to see if and when he starts missing money putts, whether he changes his putter, because as far as I know he has had the same putter for his entire playing career.

There's no point going into the various different styles of putters or saying which are the best. The two basic rules to remember are loft and weight. Yes loft, because most golfers think that all putters have no loft; wrong, they do and especially when playing on winter greens, it's better to have a putter with a bit of loft because this helps to strike the ball and keep it on top of the grass.

Have no loft for very flat summer fast greens and some loft for slow woolly winter greens.

When I used to go on regular winter golfing holidays to Spain, America etc. I always swapped my usual putter for one that had no loft and was lighter than my usual one (I expected faster greens; remember fast greens light and flat, slow greens heavy and loft).

Putting Styles

Again referring to good old Duffy Divot, his golf knowledge is not as expansive as mine and he is probably not aware of the many different putting grips and styles that are now are available to use. Most guys talking from a right handed player's perspective just grip it right hand below left.

This advice now is only for the guys suffering with their putting, if you do not, you are lucky devil!

Tip number twenty three: Try changing your hands around and place the left hand at the bottom of the grip and the right hand above. Jim Furyk and the two time Open winner Padraig Harrington use this method; it's especially effective on short putts.

Secondly there is now a new grip out called. *'The Claw Grip'.* You place your left hand at the top of the club normal grip; you place your right hand with the thumb along side of the grip facing the hole and the four fingers on the other side of the grip facing the hole, so the putter is resting between the thumb and forefinger. Masters and Open Champion Mark O'Meara, also Mark Calcaveccia, another Open Champion, both recommend this method. This advice is for the right handed players. Obviously for lefties reverse the scenario.

At the time of writing, the latest craze is the two thumb putter grip, currently being used very effectively by eight times 'Order Of Merit' winner Monty also European Ryder Cup player Miguel Angel Jimenez. It's a very wide grip which allows you to place your hands side by side with the thumbs resting against each other; this then forms a perfect triangle of your arms and shoulders.

Surprisingly most golfers play with putters that are too long for them. The industry norm is to make putters 34 or 36 inches long. They would be better using a shorter length putter, so your arms hang down naturally and are not bent at the elbows. When you have straight arms you make a much smoother stroke.

Putting is such an individualistic operation I could write a complete book on this one point of the game alone, so you will understand when I say I'll finish this chapter here, although there are still lots of other points I would like to make.

When your shot has to carry over a water hazard, you either hit one more club or two more balls.

I'm not saying I had a bad round, but I lost two balls in the ball wash.

The Day Of Reckoning

"I know I'm getting better at golf because I'm hitting fewer spectators..." Ex-President Gerald Ford

Recently I attended a meeting of 'The Comedians Golfing Society'. I am a very proud member of this prestigious show business society. I am one of its founder members and this year's Captain is our thirtieth. I had the honour of being made Captain in 1988, at this meeting I was further honoured by being made a life member. So with all this golfing experience you would think I would know how to play, after all I am trying to advise you on how to play better golf without the need to practice.

But what did I do? I broke every rule in my own book. It's no excuse but it was a very foggy and extremely cold day, so this should have told me to compensate for the weather conditions with regards to club selection etc. but did I take heed of this, I am ashamed to say no! I swung too fast trying to get extra distance in the cold weather.

To make matters worse I even gave my playing partners one of the tips from this book for playing in cold weather! To keep a similar golf ball in your pocket and play the two balls on alternative holes because a warm ball travels further than a cold one. I lost one ball after three holes, did I replace it no!

Today I was Duffy Divot; I was short of the green on every par three, as well as most of the par fours. I did take one more club, but I should have gone two clubs more, i.e. a five instead of a seven iron, or maybe when playing uphill or over bunkers three clubs up, but I didn't.

Result a very poor scoring round. I was telling my playing partners on one tee about this book, and one of my comedian friends said "The way you are playing you should read your own book", after the laughter had subsided I said "You're absolutely right".

So we all make the same common mistakes. We think we can play better than our ability. I just did not have my brain in gear that day. I have to be perfectly honest, I am, as I said in the introduction, a fair weather player. When I was younger I didn't mind the weather conditions, but now I like a nice warm sunny day.

I always play better in these conditions. I think you will agree that unless you are a complete golf nut we all play better in the warm weather. But when all is said and done I should have taken my own advice, which would have resulted in a much better round. The upside to this is like all golfers no matter what their ability, ***"Tomorrow is another day"***.

Nothing straightens out a slice quicker than a sharp dogleg to the right.

Curly, downhill, left-to-right putts are usually followed by curly, uphill right-to-left putts.

Summary

"A ball will always come to rest halfway down a hill, unless there is sand or water at the bottom..." Henry Beard

This chapter contains some observations on a few of my playing friends. Although they are not all a Duffy Divot they could all, with a few minor adjustments, improve their game.

The friends I am using now as examples enjoy playing, but because of their working commitments or their priorities, do not watch and study golf as I do. As I said at the start of this book, I am not a golf professional I am just a very keen amateur who has played a lot of golf and watched thousands of hours of golf on television. But I have not just watched. I have listened, learned and gleaned all the information I can from the best teachers and players from all over the world of golf.

I have one particular very good friend with whom I have spent many happy hours on golfing holidays, plus at home. We both belong to two very vibrant golfing societies. He was playing for many years before he met me, so why should he listen to me as to how he should play the game? I'll tell you why, because I can see what he is doing wrong. It's a fact that the best golfing teachers are ex-tour players who did not make it as top line professionals; they can then see where their fellow professionals are going wrong and try to help them. I refer to people like Butch Harman and David Leadbetter, to name just two, but there are many others. I don't for one second claim to be in their league, but it's my hobby to study the golf swing and ways of playing better golf without the hours of practice.

I want to help my friends, that's one of the wonderful things about all standards of golf. Although we all want to beat the people we are playing with, we all pass on tips and good meaning advice to our fellow players, during the round, or in the bar afterwards.

Nothing, and I mean nothing, will give me greater pleasure than to see some of my really good friends make a few minor mental and physical changes. As I have stated in the previous chapters, you do not need to have a perfect swing to score well, all you have to do is play within the capabilities of your handicap to achieve the best advantages to your score.

My friend's problem is his "address position". He addresses the ball with his arms straight out in front of him so the shaft of the club and his arms are in a complete straight line. He is a very fit guy for his age and I have known him for many years, but even his best ever tee shot has never gone further than 200 yards. You should let your arms hang down naturally from your shoulders so at the address your hands are two hands width from your groin, Take your hands, place them side by side with one hand touching your groin. Where the outside of your other hand is, that's where your hands should be 'at address' on all your golf shots, otherwise you will never develop any power.

Another friend always addresses the ball well in front of his front foot, takes the club back way on the outside and then always complains, "Why did my ball go to the right?" To make matters worse he always aims down the middle of the fairway and straight at the pin.

I have a mate who has the perfect golf swing, his practice shots are divine, but when he hits the ball he always goes at it flat out, which means his front foot slides away so he looses his balance. Result bad shot, one in ten he'll catch it great, and this is the shot he talks about for the rest of the day. The shame of it is, if he hit at the same swing tempo as his practice swing he would be, without doubt a single handicap player. He is the perfect example of the Ernie Els' swing method, 85% power result single figure handicap.

A further friend of mind is gifted with superb natural timing; he hits the ball a country mile, but all of his shots slice, which means, as he is a left-hander, he aims way right every shot. As I said earlier in this book, you can play with a slice if you use your common sense.

The point of this paragraph is, with a minor address change, he would lose that slice. He's one of these guys that says 'Don't tell me I don't want to know'; he's frightened that if he changes the swing he knows he'll lose what he's got. But he's wrong, he would be better. As I said to him once in the nineteenth hole, "you will never know until you try". Surely if he tries my suggested address position and it does not work he can always go back to his current set up.

The curse of all golfers is ***The Slow Player.*** The trouble is most slow players don't know or are not prepared to admit they are slow.

I stated earlier, golf is not a race but there are standards of play which we should all adhere to, and unduly slow play is not acceptable. These Duffy Divots are often 28 plus handicappers, which doesn't help for a start.

They take far more shots a hole than others who then are waiting on every shot. On most tees these Duffy Divots are usually the last to play, but they are never ready, they haven't got the right club or a ball out of the bag, or a glove on. They then start searching for tees etc.

Eventually on the tee they take about twenty practice swings, freeze over the ball for an eternity then take an almighty swipe and then to add insult to injury, look at their playing partners and ask "Where did that go"? Invariably it goes in the rough.

So while my playing companions and I go searching for the ball, Duffy Divot is now placing the head cover back on their club. This has to go in a precise spot in the bag, the tee in its little hole on their wife's Christmas present tee holder and they are now fifty yards behind us! If and when we find the ball, Duffy Divot then goes through the same prolonged pre-shot routine with a club totally unsuitable for the shot, like a 3 wood out 8 inch grass. So what happens, they hit it a few yards deeper into the rough, so we repeat the same scenario again, very frustrating.

I have even seen Duffy Divot take an air shot, on the rare occasion he was on a fairway, walk twenty yards to his bag and change his club. So there are times when it could be ten minutes or more before I hit my second shot. What makes matter worse is that I am now aware that we are playing slow, so I'm looking behind me and there are guys standing on the tee waiting to play, so what do I do, start rushing which gets me all out of kilter, which upsets me because I have not been the one taking all the time.

I have never had a good round when playing with a slow player. So what I am saying is be aware of your own play and be courteous to your playing partners. I'm not asking you to run around the golf course, but play at an acceptable pace. There's an old saying in golf *'Be behind the group in front and not in front of the group behind'.* All golfers should adhere to this simple rule and it would make golf so much more enjoyable.

All players should be ready to play when it's their turn, and not attempt impossible shots way above their ability. Now the next sentence could be classed as contentious. *If you can't score, please do pick up!*

But I do understand if you have paid the same money as everyone else why shouldn't you be allowed to complete eighteen holes. At the risk of repeating myself to all slow players, just be aware of your playing partners, because the most annoying thing is because you are slow everybody else speeds up and you **Mr Slow Player** never know what it's like to suffer someone else's slow play.

In conclusion, thank you for buying this book, I hope it has been of some help to you. Golf is a wonderful game; it can be both exhilarating and frustrating all at the same time.

There is one thing for sure, it's much more fun when you are playing well and hitting the little white ball from the fairway and not out of the rough.

It's a much better feeling seeing your ball sailing over the water and not saying to yourself "Bye-bye ballie".

There's a famous quotation in golf, which says, "The most important six inches in golf, are the ones between your ears".

I think this saying encapsulates all I have been tying to say. Play within your capabilities and not beyond them and you will be pleasantly surprised at how much better you will start scoring.

Enjoy your golf and I hope your drives are in the fairway and long and all your putts drop.

Good luck and remember, "Keep it on the short grass".